Mastering Negative Emotions

FELIX BAMIRIN

Other books by Felix Bamirin includes ***Forgiving Forward: The Redemption Role of the Forgiven, The Ultimate Treasure*** **and** ***Marriage on a Mission.***

This Book and other publications by the author are available at all major bookstores and book outlets nationwide.

ISBN-13: **978-1-7923-4405-3**

To the Redeeming Love, the Prince of Peace, the Bishop of our souls, the Great Physician, Jesus Christ, and the Eternal God, full of glory, grace and love, who has given us all authority and power over all things and made for us a new and living way unto perpetual victory and righteousness.

CONTENTS

PREFACE.

"We cannot control our emotional connections," a medical student from Germany touted during her presentation at a TEDx conference in May of 2018. The focus of this TEDx conference was *The Future of Society*. "We cannot control what we feel," was this presenter's apology for the normalization and acceptance of the pedophilic experience.

"It is not the fault of the pedophile that they feel what they do… it's beyond their control," she continued to argue before delving in to the true account of an associate of hers, a nineteen-year-old law student who was both a law abiding citizen, and sexually attracted to girls between the ages of six and twelve, working diligently every day to control the urge to "be himself" and act upon his emotions in a society where it is forbidden to do so legally.

In closing she offered, "…We should think about this before we judge them. We must become more compassionate and more tolerant for those who experience emotional connectivity differently than we do..."[1] This TEDx Talk has since been removed at her request, but not before it sparked a flood of controversy. She wanted it removed because she received violent death threats from emotionally charged viewers who she was certain might find her and harm her.

I reviewed some of the comments written in response to her presentation. I took notice that many people had many ideas about feelings and emotions as it pertained to behavior and what they could and could not control. Let's look at general definition for emotions here. According to Merriam and Webster, emotions are:

> *"subjectively experienced as strong feeling usually directed toward a specific object and typically accompanied by physiological and behavioral changes in the body b: a state of feeling c: the affective aspect of consciousness: FEELING [a conscious mental reaction (such as anger or fear)]*[2]

In other words, your emotions reflect your interpretation of a situation or other stimuli. Your feelings are how you decide to express your interpretation. Simply put, based on this definition alone, you do have a say in how you feel!

But, let's assume the medical student's TEDx presentation is valid and that human emotions are purely biological in nature and the dictators of our desires, beliefs, preferences and behaviors.

1 https://blog.ted.com/tedx-talk-under-review/ (paraphrased)
2 https://www.merriam-webster.com/dictionary/emotion

If human beings are incapable of controlling their emotions and feelings, invariably, our emotions and feelings control us. This would mean we are designed to live in a world where adults, who are fully developed, have no authority over their emotions and are justified in acting upon them. It's nature after all. What does this mean for our children? What does this mean for mankind?

I can recall, years ago hearing the same arguments made for same sex attracted persons. In fact, the medical student used this as justification for her argument. This medical student is not alone in her beliefs. Many people were outraged with her comments. But so many of those same people make decisions on a daily basis and chalk it up to their emotions. People claim to feel helpless when it comes to the way they feel. Rather than asking for help, they accept their feelings and emotions as a life sentence.

Now, let's assume the medical student and opinion of so many others is wrong. This means, we do have authority over our emotions. We can decide how we feel about things. We can choose how and when we want to act. If we do not like how we feel about something, we can change it. If we are feeling a certain way, we can figure out why and address the root cause and change our experience. Which of these scenarios do you want to be true?

In this book, I offer you, by the authority of the Word of God concerning our lives, that you have total agency over your emotions. We can decide to continue to justify our behaviors by our flesh and our emotions- both of which are limited and ever changing by nature, or we can choose to justify our actions in accordance with God's standard. The choice is ours.

Referring back to the medical student's presentation and the violent comments she received regarding her assertions, did you note the double standard? The same people who want their feelings tolerated could not tolerate the feelings of pedophiles, murderers, thieves, and those who criticize them for being wrong. The truth is that nobody wants to live in a world where emotions are king, and feelings are the judge of right and wrong.

Everyone is responsible for the way they feel. It is possible to create your own feelings, because they belong to us! We have authority over what we permit to incite our feelings. Knowing what to do when we feel a certain way is also our responsibility.

What if you could experience total joy, unending peace, practical faith, and live a life of perpetual victory with the ability to exert the same upon your environment creating an atmosphere of righteousness, peace, and joy for everyone around you? You would become so contagious with the overflowing joy and peace coming from your center to the rest of your life and to the people around you.

Ask anyone who has ever been without peace, they will tell you it is invaluable! Money cannot buy it. Ask the rich and famous who are suffering from mood disorders such as depression. An ever-growing relationship with Christ and the art of surrender, when mastered, makes peace a practical experience even amidst chaos.

Most people grow up accepting the lie that there is nothing they can do about their feelings and emotions, so they just let them run amuck, ruining their relationships and stifling their destiny. A life that is run by emotions will be ruined and can ruin the lives of others. There is a grand design for placing our emotions under control. You can and must learn to harness your emotions to achieve perfect peace and fulfill God's highest pleasure in this life.

The only thing that grows without any effort is weeds, not a garden full of fruits and vegetables. An understanding of the nature of man and how his emotions operate in conjunction with the other parts of the human composition will empower man to be able to put emotions in their rightful place and the spirit of man in the driver's seat again.

God made man to live by listening to the Creator and not by reasoning or relying on feelings caused by the creatures. Man was made to live by revelation and not by the senses of his own flesh. God's divine order for man at creation was altered the moment man began to make decisions on what is good or bad based on feelings rather than by the Word that proceeds from the mouth of God.

It is out of order for man to let his physical senses and emotions lead in his major life decisions, determination, actions, and relational processes. Destinies are derailed, lives destroyed, relationships severed, and a circle of unfortunate situations continue until there is a revelation of the new creation order, and kingdom provisions for processing thoughts, desires and imaginations are intentionally embraced.

The goal of this book is to create an awareness of God's divine provision for experiencing unending peace and increasing joy through knowledge. It aims to bring you into an ever-increasing flow and endless circles of peace, love and joy as it cuts short the emotional roller coasters cycle of negative feelings which breeds an atmosphere of emotional pain, hurtful passions, and vengeful intentions.

Friends, emotional mastery is possible. A Kingdom thought process is an art that can be mastered and practiced as a lifestyle. This book will feed the inner man and beckon it back to strength, authority, and control in the power of God's Spirit within.

1

A Crouching Lion.

In *Wishful Thinking*, Frederick Buechner writes that of seven deadly sins, anger is possibly the most fun. To lick your wounds... to smack your lips over grievances long past... to roll over your tongue- the very prospect of bitter confrontations still to come... to savor to the last toothsome morsel both of the pain you are given and the pain you are giving back- in many ways, it is a feast fit for a king.

The chief drawback of indulging in such a meal is that what you are wolfing down is yourself. The skeleton left drying on an empty platter after you and you enemies have consumed all, is you.[3]

There was a man named Cain. He was one of the first men

[3] Frederick Buechner, Wishful Thinking (San Francisco: Harper & Row, 1993).

ever to live; the very second generation of mankind. Being the first to experience an emotion of sadness and hate that degenerated into the first murder, Cain's emotions represent many of the emotions that will follow in the history of mankind. He was privileged to be so close to how it all began as far as the Judeo-Christian God-narrative is concerned; he had a consciousness of divinity through a firsthand encounter with God.

Cain spoke with God and worshipped Him. He was a tiller of soil who took from the abundance of his harvest as an offering and sacrifice unto God. Cain had an awareness of the supreme authority of God over man and all of man's ways, but his brother was a little more pious than he was.

Abel was a shepherd and the baby brother of farmer Cain; he loved and worshipped God as well and believed Him. As the events turned to prove, Abel was a good guy, not just by man's estimation but according to God Himself. As in many Hollywood movies, now we have a bad guy, Cain and the good guy, Abel. Even though they both started out as good guys, things happen quickly, and a good guy became a bad guy.

Cain's greatest trouble came when his emotions became his king. He cultivated his grounds quite well for a great harvest of crops, but he did not do so well with cultivating his emotions for fruit he and God could be proud of. It was not what happened, but how he handled what happened and responded to life events that became the greatest undoing for Cain.

Life is 25 percent what happens and 75 percent how we handle and respond to what happened. Cain's feelings of sadness and a downcast emotion because God was not quite as pleased with him and his offering, degenerated into the murder of his own brother. He lost control of his emotions, and thereby became the head of a generation of murderers.

Dearest destinies, visions, lives, and great potentials are being slaughtered daily because of emotions without leash. Where emotions run freely without control, endlessly reigns the death of all things dear. Marriage relationships that were designed for great kingdom missions are divorced, family relationships are disintegrated, and ministry partnerships are destroyed because of untamed emotions that are let loose to roam freely.

From simply wanting to be his brother, Cain proceeded to wishing his brother never existed. God does not show favoritism, as men do. God favors those He foreknew; He chooses with a foreknowledge and accepts those who He knew ahead of time that they would accept Him and His counsel. He knows the thoughts of the proud afar off and discerns and judges the intents of the hearts of men.

Whenever emotions roam freely and uncontrolled beware, sin is at the door and desires you like a devouring lion, but you must master it because you can and you should. This was God's caution to Cain! He was warned about the impending evil lying at his door, crouching like a lion ready for his prey, but just as a dog who would get lost by ignoring the hunter's whistles; step by step Cain wandered further away in his murderous thoughts. He hated his brother with a deep hatred until he put our good guy Abel away, down under in cruel murder.

Cain murdered his brother while they talked in the fields. He thought of Abel wickedly, but spoke to him as a friend, only to rise suddenly against him like a foe. This is a common experience in relationships generally, the betrayal of trust in business partnership, dating, marriage, and community existence. Emotions stand in the way of good judgement and many are slain in words and thoughts that continue to cry out about unfulfilled destinies and unrealized dreams. The one with whom his hand is dip in the morsel would rise up against him, the one he called a brother, with whom he fellowshipped will rise to kill him, just that thought alone in itself is killing.

And now the deed is done! Cain hid his brother's body but could not hide his voice. The voice of the blood of righteous Abel, would scream "why" in the ears of God from the depths of the earth against Cain and call day and night for justice. Negative emotions may appear as little foxes of feelings and thoughts in form, but their deeds are mighty as they do great damage to the vine. Ungoverned emotion is like rearing a lion in the home. To nurse sin in the heart is to brood vipers; in their ripened strength they would kill and not spare, they will maim and destroy. Destinies will lie in waste, visions and dreams will be slain, great and mighty strength will grind at the mills to the amusement of foes.

The goal of sin is mastery, even though it begins as though it serves one's pleasure, 'I'm at your order' it says, with murderous smiles. Once a step is yielded, it goes all the way. If we do not master our emotions and say like Jesus said, 'Begone from me, Satan', it will be a trip to the graveyard with luggage of great potentials only to live forever in the land of the forgotten. Beware of negative emotions! Watch the signals, brace yourself, and be ready because emotions must be mastered for it to serve its God-given purpose!

2

The Three in One.

No, I am not talking about the Trinity of God in this book. Rather, I am talking about man as a trinity. Man is a spirit; he has a soul and lives in a body. There are other theories that view man as a soul living in a body where the soul and the spirit are one and the same. However, I believe that there is more evidence in Scripture that confirm the former more than the latter. The soul is the seat of the mind (intellect), emotions (feelings) and the will determination/action).

The greatest commandment according to the Lord Jesus is, "Love the Lord your God with all your heart and with all your soul and with all your mind" **(Matthew 22:37)**. This means to serve, worship, glorify God, and be all about Him with your intellect, emotions, feelings, and your will. God created man to have emotions with which he can glorify God on the earth and fulfill his purpose through them. There must be a willful yielding of the mind to the honor of God. Emotions are responses to situations and information that excites and triggers it.

What you see, hear, perceive, and touch creates feelings of joy, sadness, happiness, love, anger, anxiety, or worries. The spirit is the person that came from God in the beginning who made man become a living soul through the divine breath and spirit. It is the spirit that departs when man dies while the body lays lifeless once the spirit is gone. The soul is what gives the spirit its unique personality and identity separate from other souls who are also made by the breath of God.

The consciousness of spirit outside the body is possible because of the soul. The soul is to man what a hard drive is to a computer; it is the hard drive, its capacity, and all that it contains that makes a device uniquely different from all devices of similar configuration. The soul holds all learned information and data, processes information, and determines or judges right from wrong. The spirit and the body are, however, two different sides by which information could be downloaded into the soul or the mind.

The body through the physical senses transfer information to the mind and the soul where the mind processes the information as the seat of moral judgment where right or wrong is determined in the will. Reason is what ratifies the decision of the mind, which is the intellect, and the response is sent back to the body to feel the result that information is causing to the system. Everything within the soul examines information sent in by the senses and an appropriate response is generated; it is that generated response that we understand as emotions.

Bodily action is generated on the basis of the emotion and whether that information gains enough approval. If the response generated is fear, then the body goes into flight; if the emotions is good feeling, it may generate pleasure and the body goes to engage in the activity that correlates to that good feeling.

The other channel by which the person receives information in the mind is through the awakened spirit. The Bible records that everyone born of the flesh is flesh. This means that though he is spirit, he functions without his spirit because the spirit is dead to God. As the body without the spirit is dead, so the man whose spirit does not have the influence of the Holy Spirit of God, is dead, spiritually speaking.

When a person comes to faith in Christ, what happens is that the Holy Spirit comes upon that dead spirit, makes it come alive and into a vital consciousness of God and the Spirit of Christ. He is now aware not only as flesh but as spirit. The one who had only one channel of senses now has an alternative channel of communication and information, the spiritual senses are now awakened so that he can communicate and engage in the realms of the spirit. This new man is now a new creation, possessing both physical and spiritual awareness. He is no longer limited to his physical circumstances and surroundings; he is living in a new consciousness and reality of a spiritual surrounding.

The conversion of the spirit by the regeneration of the Spirit of God happens because the soul has come to a level of yielding that permitted the entrance of the word of God and a level of understanding is gained to the point that both the mind and the will judged the Gospel as true and there is a decision in the soul that this Gospel is true and must be accepted as such; this is what believing does. The one who believes has come to understand and accept what is believed as true, and that his will now permits total surrender to that truth as the only truth by which they may now live their daily lives.

The difference between the soul and the spirit can be so subtle, so much that the Bible says that it will require the discerning ability of the Word of God as a two-edged sword to separate and divide one from the other (See **Hebrews 4:12**). The conversion of the soul sometimes takes as long you live. The soul is the faculty of man that deals with receiving and processing information for verifiable truth with reason, and the producing of decision, determination and actions because of received information.

Before a person does anything, it usually begins with a thought in the mind. The thought is the information and it is processed in the faculties of the mind, the will, and the emotions which are in the soul.

The body only does what it is told in the soul region. For example, Jesus said that every sin that a man commits begins in the heart. "For out of the heart come evil thoughts--murder, adultery, sexual immorality, theft, false testimony, slander" **Matthew 15:19**. The word "καρδίας" translated, 'heart' in the New Testament is the mind or the inner self which is the central part of a person. It is described as the manufacturing room of all human actions. It is the place where thoughts are developed and deployed as actions of the will. It is out of this heart that the issues of life spring forth and as such must be guarded with all diligence according to **Proverbs 4:23**. As a man thinks in his heart, so is he (**Proverbs 23:7**). To change a man, you must change his heart. This is the change from the inside out. Jesus compared it to making the tree good to make the fruit good. In other words, all the behavioral fruit can be controlled by changing the tree of the person's heart.

God would write his new covenant laws in the heart as compared with a stone as it was in the Old Covenant. The heart is central to God's dealing with man; God places special attention on the heart. Man looks at the outward appearance, but God looks at the heart. God judges the motives of the heart and not just actions by themselves. God rebuked the Israelites and Jesus also did the same to the Pharisees and Jews who worshipped God with their lips, but their hearts were far from God.

Worship from the heart is a precious jewel to God. The heart is the place where every true transformation begins. The body and the spirit will fall or rise dependent on what the state of the heart is. The destiny of a man is produced in the place of his heart.

3

Minding the Mind.

One interesting reality of the mind is that it is like a computer device that has the endless capacity to download and store information. Everything the eyes have seen and that the ears have heard is are all stored in the heart and mind. Movies, books, stories, impressions, suggestions, abuses, tragic events and so on, that the mind was ever exposed to don't easily disappear or get deleted but are permanently stored. Sometimes it looks like the things that the mind was exposed to have been lost, until there is a trigger that makes those things pop up again and it is called re-member-that is, a resurfacing of lost memory data stored in the mind. It was really never lost. It is stored up somewhere on the computer of the mind.

Several years ago, I accidentally deleted an audio recording I intended to use. In efforts to restore it, I searched for applications that could recover deleted files and was surprised because I got much more than I needed. I was able to recover files I have deleted long ago that I never believed could be found. I never knew that so much technology existed with the capacity to regenerate seemingly lost data from the mind of my device.

So, it is with the mind. You forget things until you encounter something related that calls it back to mind, for remembering. This is why it is so difficult most times for pornographic addictions to be broken- it works with the media of the mind that involves graphic images to be stored in the mind and any familiar image can readily bring it back up on the surface even after a person is spirit awakened and is committed to the Lordship of Jesus. Their spirit is still born again, but the mind needs a conversion which happens by renewal of the mind.

Renewing the Mind

To renew means to make something new again. It means your mind must be made new and reset or refreshed daily. It means to re-set the mind on the things above, and not on things on the Earth (**Colossians 3:2**). It means to check the thoughts, words, pictures, and things that settle on your mind more frequently and make sure they are things that are worthy of your new creation nature (**Romans 8: 1-11**).

The mind is corrupted by the world system to which it has been formerly exposed. There is a need to delete old files that have the virus, and to set the mind on a new track or course. The mind is renewed by reset; to renew the mind means to push the reset button, it is the process by which you uninstall old images and data and replace them with new images and data.

This process is about exchanging your current thoughts for the thoughts of God found in his words. It is a continual process of replacing images of hostility with the images of the love of God, images of chaos with the image of Peace, fear and doubt with faith, weakness with strength and power. It is the ability to see yourself in the mirror of the word of God and live daily adjusting yourself to the image you see. This is best described in **2 Corinthians 5:17**, "If any man is in Christ, he is a new creation, old things have passed away, behold, all things have become new".

The Unrenewed Mind

Paul described the state of the unrenewed mind in strong terms. In **Ephesians 4:17**, the Apostle claims that the mind is corrupted by the world system to which it has formerly been exposed. The mind has picked up several ideas, thoughts, feelings, and patterns of reasoning as well as behaviors and have been conditioned to respond in that manner in all of life's situations. Hence, unless you delete the old files that have been infected with the virus of sensuality, the new man will continue to struggle to walk in perpetual victory.

The mind must be set on a new track and course. The unrenewed mind walks in the ways the Gentiles walk because they have a darkened understanding. The ability of the mind to comprehend spiritual things is grossly limited in that state of mind. The more renewed the mind is, the more the ability to grasp spiritual truth increases. A mind, unrenewed, is set on carnal or earthly things and his standard of judging good and evil is impacted by earthly measures rather than the bigger picture of the spiritual dimensions of things.

The unrenewed mind is short-sighted and blind causing deadly ignorance due to the blindness of heart according to **Ephesians 4:18**. Ignorance is a destructive disease, but the good news is that through a renewed mind, it does not have to end up a terminal disease. God speaking concerning the children of Israel through the Prophet Hosea, said, "My people are destroyed for lack of knowledge" (**Hosea 6:4**).

It is not the presence of the devil or witches and wizards that destroy people, it is the lack of valuable knowledge of God and the things of God that destroy. The point of a man's ignorance is the devil's point of greatest advantage over that man. Satan's weapons of deceit work best in the arena of man's ignorance, and he will do anything to keep him that way. Renewal of the mind permits the truth to permeate through the mind. God's truth becomes your known truth, and that known truth works transformation.

The unrenewed mind is controlled and consumed by lust, uncleanness, greed, and is exposed without self-control. The Bible says that a man without self-control is like a city without walls. It is unprotected and is at the mercy of the evil one in the world. The deceitfulness of sin wearies the heart that is unrenewed until it is too weak to resist the devil and his deceptions. Paul's golden exhortation in **Romans 12:1-2** states,

> "I beseech you therefore brethren, present your bodies to God as a living sacrifice, holy and acceptable to God, which is your reasonable service. And be not conformed to the patterns of this world but be transformed by the renewing of your heart that you may prove what of that good and acceptable will of God".

The body cannot be offered unto God as a living sacrifice without a renewed mind. Worship becomes reasonable as an act of the will and of the mind that considers God worthy of everything man has to offer and give. Total transformation of spirit and body happen with the renewing of the mind. A renewed mind gives you the capacity to prove the good and perfect will of God in your life and the lives of everyone around you.

4

Emotional Mastery.

You may be familiar with IQ, that is Intelligence Quotient. Just as we have an IQ, there is also what is termed EQ or Emotional Intelligence. Emotional Intelligence is a newer concept that measures an individual's propensity for identifying and recognizing human emotions. Less discussed is Emotional Mastery- the ability to identify emotions, harness and manage one's emotions, as well as the management of emotions by others through subjecting them to kingdom life and principles.

Emotional mastery gives us an advantage over our emotions so that we are truly in charge of how our emotions are used to express our unique personalities and our God-given purposes. Without emotional mastery, the emotions run as they come and lead the owner into dangerous, uncharted paths. Emotional mastery is what puts us in charge of our own emotions. Emotions are generally blind, to let them run without control is like letting a beloved blind friend drive with you in the car. Emotions are responses and not causes; they do not just happen on their own, but something triggers them and makes them happen. This is because emotions have no will of their own. Emotions will run even when they are tricked into existence.

Real fear in response to an unreal threat is a common human experience. For instance, you may be sitting in a dark part of your house and be totally calm until someone tells you they saw a snake in that corner earlier that day. You'll probably jump up in fear and your peace party in that corner is over for many days. The snake story was made up and not real at all, but because emotion is blind, it does not know the difference. Your emotions were already running though there wasn't really anything lurking in your peaceful, dark corner. This is how emotions are. They will respond to anything the brain chooses to believe.

The believer not only worships and honors God in their spirits, they worship and honor God in their soul as well. We must love and serve the Lord with all our minds and hearts. As we surrender all of our lives to God and yield our will to the Lordship of Jesus, we must consciously begin to yield our emotions in total surrender unto God and submit them to the Lordship of Christ.

Name It + Tame It

Emotional Mastery includes the ability to identify and name one's emotion; this is emotional awareness. What you can name, you can tame; the ability to identify and name one's emotions gives the first power and control over it and is a diagnosis in a way. A professional auto mechanic does not start to fix a broken car without first running a diagnosis. The aim of a diagnosis is first being able to name it; it helps to be able to identify personal emotions. If you name it, you can face it, and once you face it you will tame it.

In naming the emotion, you do not try to excuse it or dress it up looking like what you want it to be rather than what it truly is. If it is sadness, identify it as such. If it is shame, call it so. If it is a negative emotion, keep it in that category until you can identify the positive direct opposite emotion to it. There are core emotions that are biologically determined, emotional responses and their expressions are just the same for everyone regardless of their ethnic or cultural backgrounds. These responses do not depend on what part of the world you live in and which kind of culture you grew up in.

Harness + Assign It

The next task of emotional mastery is to be able to harness emotions and apply them to achieve desired goals and outcomes. Harnessing emotions helps to apply them to specific tasks like spiritual thoughts and problem-solving activities. To harness something is like putting a harness on a horse or other draft animal, or it means to control and make use of natural resources to produce energy. Emotions are like a wild horse that must be harnessed in order to enjoy the purpose for which a horse is created and used. Emotions are also like natural resources that must be put under control and processed to achieve greater usefulness and effectiveness, like people harness the wind to produce electricity.

Once the emotion is identified, the next step is to subject this emotion to a spiritual thought process. This thought process is not a thought in the head, but a thought in the regenerated heart. The head thought process will only aggravate and not alleviate the emotions. You must learn to subject your emotion to the thoughts of God within your heart. This is where you subject all dark pictures your emotions are painting in the canvas of your heart to the light, and negative images are processed into positive, beautiful, kingdom images.

Most emotional outbursts happen because emotions are generally hasty, so they are not patient with kingdom thought patterns. Kingdom thought processes are usually too slow and too Christ-focused for emotional outbursts. Emotional outburst are what damages destinies and disintegrate destiny relationships. The goal of emotional mastery is to find the best, most appropriate expression for the emotion to prevent an outburst that may be

unproductive and destructive. It is not the goal of emotional mastery to only suppress the emotion, but to dominate it in order to find a healthy expression for it in God-honoring and glorifying ways. Harnessing emotions joins the emotional process to the kingdom thought process, where emotions are identified, connected to its source, and committed to a kingdom process for problem solving and for godly impact.

Vital questions for harnessing emotions include: What is the source of this emotion? Why do I feel the way I feel right now? What makes this feeling different from other feelings? How do I achieve my goals with this feeling? Are there alternative ways by which I could express this emotion apart from the ways I am used to? What will be the result if choose this mode of expression or if I choose another possible mode of expression? How would the Holy Spirit vent through this emotion? How did Jesus do it? What would Jesus say and do right now?

This kingdom thought process is what puts the owner of the emotion in charge rather than the emotion itself. The thought process slows down the possibility of outbursts and creates tasks to which the emotion may be assigned. The focus is shifted from the self-satisfying outcomes to a God-glorifying outcome. This is how to yield your emotions to God as a channel of the fruit of the Spirit.

Master + Manage It

The final task of emotional mastery is to manage the emotions. As you identify the emotion and engage it in the thought process by applying it to a specific task and purpose, you will be regulating your emotions and develop the ability to help others to do the same. Regulating means that you are not just achieving one-time success with your emotion, but you are forming a new and consistent way of dealing with emotions on a regular basis.

One cannot be said to have mastered anything unless they have been able to produce the same kinds of results consistently. Mastery is not just knowing how to do it but knowing how to repeat the system to produce the same result over and over again. Hence, it begins with a conscious practice and being aware of the possibilities and tendencies of emotions and choosing to be responsible for expressing them in ways that befits the new nature of the new man in Christ. At this level of mastery, one is also able to help others to do the same. There are people who know how to play a certain musical instrument who may not be able to teach that skill to other people.

Mastery is more than knowing what to do and how to do it, but knowing what to do, understanding how to do it, and the wisdom to teach others how to do it for the same result without fail. Emotional mastery must be done with the consciousness of the presence of Christ within and the continual awareness of the power of the Holy Spirit within. The Holy Spirit within the believer brings forth fruit of the Spirit which is summed up in love. It is one fruit with multiple functions (**Galatians 5:22-23**).

Dennis and Jennifer Clarke in their Book, '*Flowing in the River of God's Will*', puts this in a very beautiful way:

- **Joy is love rejoicing |** We find pleasure in God's presence.
- **Peace is love ruling |** We are under the Lordship of Jesus Christ.
- **Patience is love enduring** | We are willing to wait for God's timing.
- **Kindness is love giving |** We serve others with mercy.
- **Goodness is love motivating |** Our heart is moved by love and holiness.
- **Faith is love trusting |** We can believe God and others can believe us.
- **Gentleness is love esteeming**| We "esteem others better" than ourselves (Philippians 2:3).

- **Self-control is love retraining|** We are "kept by the power of God" (I Peter 1:5).[4]

Emotional mastery is perfected when our emotions become the expression of the fruit of the Spirit rather than erratic expressions of the baggage of self.

4 Dennis & Jennifer Clark, Flowing in the River of God's Will: Your Place of Effortless Trust & Perfect Peace. Destiny Image Publisher, Shippensburg, 2018.

5

More than Just Emotions.

The experience of emotions is a natural instinctive state of mind deriving from one's circumstances, mood, or relationships with others. Instinctive or intuitive feelings as distinguished from reasoning or knowledge, emotions can be feeling, sentiment, passion, reaction, or sensation.[5]

Emotions are a response to stimulus; they are induced and triggered. According to Wikipedia, emotions are "biological states associated with the nervous system brought on by neurophysiological changes variously associated with thoughts, feelings, behavioral responses, and a degree of pleasure or displeasure".[6] While emotions are neurophysiological and biological, they are also spiritual. They are spiritual because they have spiritual implications.

5 "Emotion" Oxford Languages. Lexico, www.lexico.com.
6 "Emotions" Wikipedia. Wikimedia Foundation. Accessed 07/02/2020. en.m.wikipedia.org

Emotions emit signals and create an atmosphere for spirits to operate. They can even be contagious such that everyone in the room is infected. Negative emotion are like a stench. Flies need no invitation. They automatically gravitate toward it. Demons have the same connection with negative emotions. Paul warns, "and give no foothold to the devil" (**Ephesians 4:27**). This is an instruction coming right along with the instruction to never let the sun go down on your anger. Anger and other negative emotions attract demonic presence and give them the legal ground of operation in an atmosphere where they thrive.

Demonic oppressions are mostly expressed in the realm of emotions before they are translated to physical actions. The mood by which demons express themselves is in the realm of the soul where they are able to manipulate their hosts to behave in a manner not consistent with the host's normal behavior.

Anger

According to the King James Version Dictionary, anger is:

"...a choke strangle, vex; vexation, anguish, the quinsy, angina. It means to strangle, to strain or draw together to vex. The primary sense is to

press, squeeze, make narrow; The Hebrew meaning means to strangle.[7]

The KJV Dictionary further defines anger as, "a violent passion of the mind excited by a real or supposed injury; usually accompanied with a propensity to take vengeance, or to obtain satisfaction from the offending party"[8]. The Bible warns against the prolonged emotion of anger because of its propensity to revenge an offense.

Anger should be expressed and not repressed, but it must be expressed in a way that does not cause one to sin. Forgiving, love, and peace are the positive alternatives and kingdom atmosphere that the kingdom person ought to set their mind on.

Sadness

Sadness is an emotional pain associated with or characterized by feelings of disadvantage, loss, despair, grief, helplessness, disappointment, and/or sorrow. Sorrow is the absence of joy. Joy is a fruit of the Spirit and is one of the signs of the atmosphere of God's kingdom. The kingdom of God is not a matter of eating and drinking but righteousness, peace and joy in

7Anger" King James Version Dictionary, KJVD. Accessed 07/02/20. www.av1611.com

8 Ibid.

the Holy Ghost (**Romans 14:17**).

Life happens every day from a loss of a job, failed expectations, heart breaks, death, and all manner of circumstances that may cause deep sorrow.

Joy

No one has to stay sorrowful all of their days, though; there is a remedy in the Holy Spirit, it is joy. Joy is not the feeling you get when something good happens, it is a weapon we need in order to stay in the victory that Jesus won for us and to stay in the victory Jesus won for us. Amidst whatever circumstance of life that we face, joy is a decision to be made in order to usher in the atmosphere of the Kingdom for Kingdom miracles and encounters. Paul and Silas were shackled hand and foot in prison after they were arrested for casting out a money-making demon from a servant girl.

They had every reason to emit sadness in their emotions, but by the revelation of the joy principle they chose rather to worship God in prayer and sing songs of praise. As there are triggers for negative emotions, there are also triggers for positive kingdom emotions as well: Joy is triggered in praise and songs of worship.

The apostles understood the principle of not allowing your

circumstance to enslave your emotions and trigger aromas that invite demons, therefore they practiced it in the most unlikely moments of their lives and taught it as well. Paul wrote, "Rejoice in the Lord always. I will say it again, Rejoice!" (**Philippians 4:4**). The emphasis is not for a palliative measure, but rather a real life of rejoicing that must be cultivated consciously through the Holy Spirit's strength.

Doubt

Doubt is a feeling of uncertainty and lack of conviction. It is the state of being double minded. Doubt is a lack of, and the opposite of, faith. Many great destinies have been buried because of doubt. Someone refuses to take a bold step because they are unsure of themselves and of their potential. They doubt everything including God. They move six steps forward and seven steps backward until they lose all opportunity to know God, see God's mighty wonders that are tied to their faith, but if only they would believe! This again is one of Satan's weapon to puncture the faith building process.

Doubt is Satan's question mark where God's period is. Did God really say that you should not eat from any of the trees in the Garden? God had already completed the instruction with a statement of command, but Satan subtly came to Eve and mislead her feelings in the path of doubt. He succeeded in planting doubt where convictions once resided. Doubting is questioning the finality of God's word and the principles of God that require a hundred percent conviction for them to be activated.

Faith

Faith is the opposite of doubt and faith that is built upon the promises of God to us in Christ Jesus! We must let every fiber of our being say "yes" and "amen" to every promise God made to us, because in Christ that is exactly what they are; yes, and amen. Done! There is no room for doubts anymore.

Hatred

Hatred is intense dislike and ill-will towards something or someone. John equated hatred with murder. He said, "whosoever shall hate his brother is a murderer: and ye know that no murderer hath eternal life abiding in him" (**1John 3:15**). Love is the Kingdom version of the emotion of hate. The believer does not just love, the believer is love.

In regeneration, the believer is *regened* to carry the DNA of God, so because God is love, the believer is love. Love is a major quality that gives a believer away. Jesus said, "*By this shall all men know that you are my disciples if you have love for one another"* **(John 13:35)**. Love is who we are and what we are loaded with daily. The Bible says that the Holy Spirit in us and sheds the love of God abroad in our hearts. This gun is loaded with love bullets, and that is what it shoots every time the trigger is pulled.

There should be absolutely no hate or disgust in us toward anyone. We must be quick to renew our mind anytime we sense that hate is lurking in our heart so that we can master it before it has us. The package of hate may be brought to our door, but we have enough seed of love so that we do not take delivery of it; we will not sign to accept the delivery because it does not belong in our heart nor in our house. God, who is love is already resident in our house and hearts.

Anxiety | Worry

Anxiety is a feeling of worry, nervousness, or unease about an imminent event or something with an uncertain outcome. Anxiety is feeling apprehensive and losing inner peace concerning issues and people over which you have absolutely no control. It is usually triggered by a sense of losing control. It is the direct opposite of the peace. Jesus is the Prince of Peace and he promises peace to his disciples despite the unpredictable future to which he has called them. Jesus, said, "In the world you will have tribulation but in me you have peace, be of good cheer, I have overcome the world" **(John 16:33)**.

Your location determines your apprehension. In the world, tribulation is inevitable and in Christ, peace is inevitable. Peace instead of anxiety comes, when we know we may not be in control, but there is no loss of control because God who neither sleeps nor slumber is the sustainer of the Universe and He is always in control of our lives, our future, and our eternal destiny.

We may not be in control, the one who holds us is in control. Tomorrow is in his hands and he works all things together for our good. He does not need us to deputize Him in matters of the control of the Universe, He is the Maker and Sustainer of all things; he holds all things by the power of His.

Someone once said, I may not know what tomorrow holds, but I know Him who holds tomorrow. This is the assurance that calms our anxiety always. Jesus doesn't want us to be anxious about tomorrow, what we will eat, or what we will wear because he wants us to trust God for the provision of those things that we need while we focus on seeking His Kingdom and His righteousness. To worry about those things means we will have to abandon seeking the kingdom. So instead of praying, "Thy Kingdom come, and thy will be done on earth as it is in heaven", we will be seeking bread.

According to the Model Prayer, once we have prayed, "Give us this day our daily bread", we should trust the heavenly Father to do just that. He will daily load us with benefits, and our experience with Him today is what guarantees that He will do it again. Trust is eroded in anxiety. It is the most practical way of passing a vote of no confidence on the government of His peace. We must serve God and draw near to Him with confidence and the full assurance of faith, doubting nothing because the one who doubts in the Kingdom is a poor man. He is destitute of faith, which is kingdom currency which you must exchange for all that the Kingdom has to offer.

Fear

Fear is a distressing emotion aroused by real or imagined impending danger, evil, or pain. It is the feeling or condition of being afraid. The most dangerous of all emotions is fear. Fear does not originate from God; He clearly disowns fear when His word says, "For God has not given us the spirit of fear, but of power, and of love, and of a sound mind" (**2 Timothy 1:7**). The acronym for fear has been described by someone as False Evidence Appearing Real. Fear is an instrument of worship; what you fear has your focus, and what has your focus you worship.

Jesus said, do not fear man who can kill the body and after that can do no more. But I will show you who to fear, fear Him who after he has killed the body can cast both the body and the soul into hell (**Matthew 10:28**). Fear is an acknowledgement of worth and power of what or who is feared. Evil is attracted to the fear of it. The Psalmist knew that so well when he said, "Yea though I walk through the valley of the shadow of death, I will fear no evil for thou art with me" (**Psalm 23:4**).

Evil loves to be feared, but God is the only One who is worthy to be feared and adored. Job lamented that what he feared most had befallen him (**Job 3:25**). The Bible declares that we were all subject to bondage because of the fear of death (**Hebrews 2:15**). The fear of death brings death, but the fear of God draws the Presence of God near us. Godly fear does not bring panic, it is a reverent fear that we give to God. It is how we express acknowledgement of God, His majesty, power, and grace. Job was always offering sacrifices for the sins of his children and said, perhaps they have sinned against God lest they were struck dead by God. But then that is exactly what happened.

Obedience is indeed better than sacrifice. Fear only God, do not fear death or it will come and before it comes, it will first hold you in a long bondage. The righteous, the Bible says, are as bold as lion. **Psalms 27** declares so powerfully, "The Lord is my light and salvation whom shall, I fear? The Lord is the strength of my life, of whom shall I be afraid?" When God is in His rightful place in our hearts, fear will not wander around for anything else in and around us.

Shame

Shame is a painful sensation excited by a consciousness of

guilt, or of having done something which could injure a reputation. Shame is particularly excited by the disclosure of actions which, in the view of men, are mean and degrading. It is often therefore manifested by a downcast look or by blushes or a face of confusion.[9]

The first experience of shame in the Bible was after the fall of Adam and Eve. It was clearly stated that even when the two strangers met each other for the first time as husband and wife, that they were both naked and were not ashamed. But as soon as they disobeyed God by eating of the tree of knowledge of good and evil, they saw that they were naked because their eyes were opened, and they started to feel ashamed. It was shame that led Adam and Eve to devise a means to hide themselves with leaves. This confirms the fact that emotional feelings are connected to spiritual status.

Emotions will enjoy peace when God is in his rightful place in someone's heart, whereas the same person will feel shame and guilt because of not being in the right place. A wrong place, spiritually speaking, is not always in a place of sin, but it can be a place of ungodly friendships and relationships. A wrong place can also be in a place of lack of knowledge of who one is and the big picture of how God views that person. The wholeness of the person is important to the spirit, soul, and the body. When one part of a human is sick, the whole part is impacted negatively.

9 Shame. KJV Dictionary. AV1611.com Accessed 07/02/2020. www.av1611.com

6

Emotional Triggers.

Every gun has a trigger. A loaded gun does not go off unless the trigger is pulled. Everyone is like a loaded gun with all manners of bullets loaded in the mind right from childhood. Every childhood trauma of abuse, failed experiences, parent's divorce, bullying, wrong self-image, negative projections, loss of loved ones, and all other events and circumstances of life always load up a bullet in us. So, people grow up as victims of their circumstances and servants of past traumatic events of their early, middle, or 'anytime' years.

They walk around looking innocent and nice but carrying around hurts like baggage or worse, like loaded guns. Everything seems alright until the trigger is pulled, and they shoot all manner of emotional outbursts. Many times, the current issue is not really the main issue in emotional expressions, this is only the trigger issue. Other issues have loaded or rather have been pre-loaded into the mind with bullets that are now shooting forth unhappiness, fear, doubt, anger, and anxiety and all other outbursts of emotions.

Most destructive emotional outbursts are just the final straws and tipping points, the cumulative effect of all the incidents in life that the mind has loaded as bullets that are now going off and the current incidents are just the triggers. Everyone has different triggers for different emotions. A meowing cat may signal disgust in some while it will trigger love in most cat lovers. An approaching deadline may trigger excitement in some while it may trigger anxiety or panic in others.

Emotional mastery is the ability to learn those triggers and how to either avoid them or how to cope with them without allowing them to shoot at the wrong time and at the wrong people or things. Hurting people hurt people. The people who carry the wounds of past trauma end up hurting innocent people that come across their path.

Emotional triggers are connected to past experiences from which many people are never truly healed. They had a regenerated spirit as believers, but they lack a converted soul. The image of God is imprinted upon the spirit of the regenerated man, but it is through the sanctification process that the image of God and of Christ is fully formed in the soul of the believer, so that they now function as one who has the mind of Christ and not just the Spirit of Christ.

From the moment of salvation onward there is an ongoing work of sanctification by the Spirit that seeks to delete your old files and to replace them with new files that are from Zion, the city of God. The salvation of the soul is the goal of your faith according to Peter (**1 Peter 1:9**). You do not only look like God in your spirit which does not appear, but you look like God in your soul for a visible, tangible expression in the earth. The triggers remain like a remote-control to the device of your mind.

The goal is to separate your device (your mind) from the controlling influence of the triggers of early life traumas and so on by getting your mind off the same frequency as the remote-control of bad and negative experiences. Triggers will still be pulled but the mind does not respond anymore like before. It may be a long, tedious process, but with the help of and submission to the Holy Spirit and the principles of God's Kingdom, it is very easily attainable. It is a process that involves much time and relentless exercise in godliness.

A songwriter once wrote this song:

I'm not moved by what I see, Halleluiah!
I'm not moved by what I hear, Halleluiah!
I'm not moved by what I feel, Halleluiah!
I'm only moved by the Word of God
Hallelujah! (2x)

Here is the deal, you can rightly take your mind off the same frequency of the remote-control system of pain, past regrets, guilt, shame, all other associated images of sin, and all past experiences that continue to wedge strong negative influence on the mind. There is a new reconfiguration of the mind to make it follow the frequency of the words and thoughts of God. The Word of God, the principles of the Kingdom, and the thoughts of God now become new triggers and a remote-control for the mind.

The mind is loaded with an adequate amount of the Word of God and godly bullets, so that when the trigger is pulled, it is love bullets that shoot instead of hate; joy instead of sadness. The Psalmist says in **Psalms 16:8**, "I have set the Lord always before me. Because He is at my right hand, I will not be shaken". What moves the emotion within you is connected to what you have set before you always.

The only one who can move you when the Lord is the one you set before you always, is the Lord. The only one who has the remote-control of your emotions and destiny is God whom you have set before you always. What you have not set in your mind and thoughts always will lose its power over your mind, emotions, and will. It cannot move you or excite your emotions. We have a responsibility to set the Lord always before us in the daily, night and day meditation upon the Word of God and keeping the same in our mouth in faith confession and declaration.

Just as the negative events of the past have taken over our thoughts and meditation and passion, we must give our affection, passion, and time to cultivating a new culture of mind and heart, meditating upon the Lord. Setting your affection or mind on things above and not on things below according to **Colossians 3:2** is an intentional effort and a spiritual exercise. While this Scripture refers to spiritual things by things above, and earthly things as things below, we can also safely interpret this to be an instruction and encouragement to set our mind intentional on things that we can aim at on top and not down on things that are beneath us far below our identity in Christ.

So many things are now beneath the new creation status of the believer. The things that kept the head down perpetually, they are below and in the earth realms. The child of God must aim higher for things that befits their new status. Righteousness, peace, and joy in the Holy Ghost are the things worth pursuing passionately now. They are worth keeping the mind on perpetually.

7

Mastering Emotions God's Way.

Cain became a symbol of negative emotions. **1 John 3:12** says, we should not be like Cain, who belonged to the evil one and murdered his brother. Why did he murder him? Because his actions were evil and his brother's actions were righteous.

The Cain Complex

Let's pay close attention to Cain's character traits. Who did he turned out to be?

- **He became a Satanic vessel**. Cain allowed himself to be possessed or owned by the devil. He became an instrument of Satan. He lent his soul and then his body to Satan for use to murder his own brother and terminate God's purpose for Abel, who was righteous.

- **He became a murderer.** Murder is a very grave sin because it involves putting an end to a life that God originated. Human life is so sacred only God gives it, no one has the right to take it.

- **He became a general evil doer.** It was not only in his action of murder that Cain did evil. He also became a perpetual evil doer. After jealousy, he killed. After murder, he lied about his brother's whereabouts.

- **He became the enemy of righteousness.** Cain became the enemy of that which is good. More so, he became a killer of the one he should keep.

How Good Things Become Evil

In **Genesis 4:1** Eve says, "I have begotten a man (Cain) by the help of the Lord". Over time her statement has been interpreted by translators to mean several different things. One translation says, "I have brought forth a man... the Lord!" This suggests she thought she had actually given birth to the Messiah, the Lord, who would crush the Serpent's head according to the promise in **Genesis 3:15**. Based on this point of view, the parents were excited. Even the name they chose expressed great expectation of this other man apart from Adam, who was now there with great possibilities.

There was a sense of relief in the name Cain, that suggests she had gotten this newborn by the help of the Lord. All that excitement was short-lived when this man Cain would not live up to his name by continually depending on the help of the Lord in managing his emotions. What was gotten with the help of the Lord now became an instrument in the devil's hand to destroy. This reveals the importance of discipleship in achieving total transformation of body, soul, and spirit.

The two boys, Cain and Abel, had a God- consciousness growing up like most children who are born and raised in the church today. They offered sacrifices, but obviously Cain wasn't doing something right with that God-consciousness. Spiritual activity that becomes religious activity ends up becoming a frustrating and emotional drain for many rather than an uplifting spiritual exercise. Cain lacked the understanding of the faith process because he was obviously engrossed with the Law of works which was what the Adamic covenant was built upon which the Mosaic Law would later capture on tablets.

The Law of works was built upon, "out of every tree of the Garden, you may freely eat, but out of the tree of the knowledge of good and evil you must not eat, for the day you eat of it, you shall surely die". This is a work and reward religious system which based life on the ability to keep a rule which you are not capable of keeping for too long.

This is the unfortunate religious system on which most of the religions of today are still being built. People are therefore trying so hard to meet and fulfill what they could never fill fully. The reward systems that claim you will only be given what you deserve leaves men ever pursuing what they could never fully and truly attain only to be frustrated and emotionally devasted and destructive.

As we see Abel enter into the hall of faith list of the Hebrews writer, we saw the difference between Abel and Cain: the reason Abel's offering was accepted and not Cain's, and why God had regard for Abel and his offering, but no regard for Cain nor his offering was faith! By faith, Abel offered a more excellent sacrifice than Cain, by which he obtained witness that he was righteous, God testifying of his gifts…"and by it he, being dead yet speaketh"[10].

My Sunday school class as a child, or maybe every Sunday school class, teaches that it was because Cain brought the worst part of his harvested farm products; the rotten tomatoes and poor looking grains and so on. Some claim that it was because Cain's offerings were not blooded things, but we see that God would, by Himself command the people to bring grain offerings to him in Leviticus which means that God wasn't concerned about the offering being blooded!

God's favor is not based upon man's labors; Cain only needed to have faith in God. The offering is not God's main focus but the heart with which they are offered, whether they are full of faith and trust in God or just full of fear and self; who you are

10 Hebrews 11:4

which informs what you do consistently are God's ultimate focus. Remember, God looks at the heart before he would look at your hand. If your heart is pure, your hands will be. He wants you more than he wants anything from you. If you're not acceptable, your offering won't be either.

Cain's Downward Road

God graciously warned Cain not about his unacceptable offering but his countenance and emotions. God proved to Cain that He had no respect of persons, "...If you do well, will you not be accepted? If you practice what is right consistently, you will get a right result consistently" **(Genesis 4:7).** To do well did not mean work harder because Cain worked. He brought an offering of what he had based on his profession as a tiller of the ground, but what he needed to do well was what Abel did, give an offering of faith!

There are so many times that well-meaning believers do everything they know to do to please the Lord, but the most important thing in pleasing God, they leave undone. It is impossible to please God without faith. You may give a million dollars and a million-dollars' worth of service out of fear, pride, doubts, self-confidence, self-promotion. In other words, you may do good things in wrong ways.

Cain's focus was himself; he was more concerned about being accepted than worshipping the One to whom the offering was being offered. This is evident in how angry he became about not being accepted that he would kill the one that was accepted even when that would not make him accepted. He was a giver but not a worshipper. He gave for the wrong primary motive: to be accepted. This is a downward emotional slope for anyone.

Relationships: Put the First Thing First

An effective relationship is not primarily articulated by acceptance. It feels good to accept and be accepted, but the first priority in meaningful relationships is love. Relationships are first and foremostly about love. The willingness to give and bless. The willingness to sacrifice for the good of the other person even when it comes at your cost.

Those who give to be accepted continue to get hurt and to hurt others. There are countless stories of girls who will give sex so they could be accepted. There are women who will give and give in their relationships to be accepted by their spouse. It usually is the case that the partner never gets to respect them or honor them for who they are.

Any relationship that you must initiate by gift you will have to sustain with gifts, and any relationship you sustain with gift is no relationship. Relationships must be about mutual commitment with mutual respect and a sense of worth. Cain's first step towards becoming an emotional wreck was his obsession with acceptance.

We must never let the desire for acceptance become a major factor in our relationships, but let value and worth drive them. It should be more about how willing you are to serve the needs of others according to your estimate of their worth. A brother is worth more than an unacceptable sacrifice, or a failed business, or an unmet expectation.

The Danger of Cain's Kind of Anger

Anger is one of the emotions that led Cain down the road to destruction. There is room for anger, but prolonged anger is a like riding in a car without breaks! It will ride well until the breaks are needed and then a crash becomes inevitable. Therefore, the Scripture warns, "be angry but sin not, let not the sun go down on your anger".

Anger is not meant to be bottled up; it is meant to be expressed. When anger is bottled up, it leads to resentment and resentment is a timed bomb! Anger is a potential doorway to sin. So, anger must be dealt with as quickly as necessary because if it stays for too long, it will birth sin (**Ephesians 4:26**). Anger is a signal that sin is around, that an atrocity or a crime is about to be committed.

Anger is also a response to an already suffered offense or wrongdoing, but it might create a circle of offense that must be stalled at some point before it generates a circle of heinous behavior and tendencies. Anger separates us from the people we want to be near us, and it shatters intimacy. So, the warning to Cain was golden and it is to the generation that would like to function in the spirit of Cain, "sin is at your door" but you must master it.

8

The Dangers of Unmastered Emotions.

There is at least one Cain in every modern city. There may even be one in every organization, family and even every church family. The following was reported in 1994 in a study conducted by the Gallup Organization:

> "Philadelphia ranked the first among U.S. cities on what was called the "hostility index.' The hostility index was based on a nine-question scale that asked people how they felt about such things as loud rock music, supermarket checkout lines, and traffic jams. Other cities on the hostility top five were New York, Cleveland, Chicago, and Detroit. At the bottom of the hostility index were Des Moines, Minneapolis, Denver, Seattle, and Honolulu. Medical experts looking at the results felt it was no coincidence that the cities that rated high on the hostility index also had higher death rates. Commenting on the study, Dr. Redford Williams of Duke University Medical School said, "Anger kills. There is a strong correlation between

hostility and death rates. The angrier people are and the more cynical they are, the shorter their life span"[11]

Mastering the Emotions

A wild horse needs to be harnessed and 'broken' for effective usefulness. Emotions, like a wild horse must be broken and tamed. Unbroken and untamed emotions will continue to run wild and cause much damage and destruction everywhere until a decision to break it and tame it is made.

Set Your Alarms

Wouldn't it be a great idea to have an alarm that goes off when emotions are about to cause some very devastating events in your life and around you? The good thing is that there is such an alarm; it is in you as the voice of conscience. In a believer, it is the voice of the Holy Spirit within. Your alarm must be maintained with regular intake of the Word of God, that is, the Bible. There is no point having an alarm that has no battery in it

11 "Philadelphia, New York Rank 1-2 in Survey of Hostile Communities", Christian Reader, September/October 1995, page 42.

and is not turned on. There is also no point in admiring an alarm that will not set for it to go off at the right time and sensitize you to the matters you have set it for. God's voice was the alarm for our man Cain, but he hit the snooze button every time until finally the alarm turned off! Eric Zorn writes in the Chicago Tribune about a tragic accident that shows the terrible power of unmastered emotions:

According to Zorn, a man and a woman were driving a van in the far-left lane of Chicago's Northwest Tollway in April 1994. In the back were two children. A white Cadillac driven by an ex-convict suddenly pulled up behind them, tailgating mere inches from their bumper. The man driving the van slowed down. The Cadillac pulled into the right lane, passed the van, so suddenly that the van driver felt he had to swerve to avoid a collision. The white Cadillac sped away. But the van driver accelerated and gave it a chase. He eventually pulled alongside the white Cadillac and reportedly began yelling and screaming. According to a witness, the two men gestured angrily at each other. The driver of the Cadillac then pulled a handgun and fired at the van. The bullet entered the side of the van and hit the baby girl, entering under her left ear and exiting above her right ear. The little girl lived, but she is blind in one eye, half blind in the other, partially deaf, and suffers severe mental and physical disabilities. The man who fired the bullets is in jail and the parents of the little girl must now live with the terrible pain of regret. Anger usually escalates often in tragic, tragic ways.[12]

That is why God warned Cain and said, "sin is at your door". What is usually at the door is more than just sin, but sin and its entourage of attendant tragic consequences! Sin's desire is for man, not his acceptability or his offering. There is a battle for the soul and the destiny of man. Emotions are more than just a fleeting moment of misbehavior; it can be a moment of activating a lifetime of eternal consequences.

The Sin of Progression

James says, "Let no man say when he is tempted, I am tempted of God: for God cannot be tempted with evil, neither tempteth he any man: But every man is tempted, when he is drawn away of his own lust, and enticed. Then when lust hath conceived, it bringeth forth sin: and sin, when it is finished, bringeth forth death" (**James 1:13**).

Pay attention to the way sin works. There are many people who throw their hands in the air helplessly when it comes to matters of the sin that besets them. They feel like it just happens,

12 Eric Zorn, "In Traffic Disputes, Turn Away and Live," Chicago Tribune, 8 November 1994, sec. 2, p.1.

and they cannot help it. Sometimes, they end up blaming the devil or God for causing them to do what they do.

There are believers who also submit to deliverance after deliverance and prayer after prayer in a bid to put an end to the circles of sin in their lives. The Scripture has an answer to how and where to begin the fight against sin. The struggle against sin is real. It is inherent in every man because of original sin. However, Jesus Christ became sin and destroyed the power of sin in the lives of all who believe so that now, sin has no dominion or power over them any longer.

Romans 6:14 says, "Sin is no longer your master, for you no longer live under the requirements of the law. Instead, you live under the freedom of God's grace. For sin shall not have dominion over you: for ye are not under the law, but under grace". This comes with the reality of the new creature in Christ. Through participation in the death, burial, and resurrection of Jesus Christ, the believer is set free from the power, penalty, and presence of sin.

However, just as it is possible for Jesus to get off his cross because it was in his power to do so, but rather he submitted himself willingly to that death on the cross; the believer, who is dead to sin and alive to righteousness in Christ, is also capable in his flesh to sin and yield his members again as instruments of unrighteousness to fulfill the evil desires of his flesh. So, James says, God is not responsible for anyone's sin. God has given the believer the ability to say no to ungodliness and worldly passion through the grace of the Lord Jesus Christ.

God doesn't tempt anyone to sin. Satan, who is the tempter, also only tests based on the desires of every man. This explains why Jesus was tempted only at an opportune time by Satan. The opportune time recorded in Scripture was when Jesus had a desire caused by hunger for food which led to other temptations in that series. According to James, every man is tempted when he is drawn away in his own lusts or desires. Every thousand steps in sin's direction begin with a single step of lust or desire. A desire for fame, for pleasure, or position or power, becomes a fertile zone for sin to be implanted and conceived.

James used the analogy of conception as in the animal reproductive system. It is like the picture of the ovum, the mature female reproductive cell and the male cell. The ovum will come and go when there is no male cell to fertilize it. But as soon as it is fertilized, it becomes an embryo, and once an embryo, there will surely be a delivery of a baby.

The baby of sin is made in the same way. The ovum is the desire; sin must be conquered at the level of desire. Every lingering desire risks the potential of being fertilized by the opportune time and chance, and once that happens, desire conceives and brings forth sin and sin brings forth death. Sin must be controlled from the doorway. If you cannot see sin before it is conceived, you will always produce a sin child only to regret it after.

Emotions have triggers. If a man can master the things that trigger sin, he will master sin at the door before an entrance is gained into his life. Whoever is in control of the doorway will control all responses and whoever controls all responses governs the life of a person. We can either respond according to the Law of the Spirit of life in Christ or we can respond according to the law of sin and death.

9

The Law of the Spirit of Life.

The battle between the flesh and the spirit of the born-again believer of the gospel of Jesus Christ is vividly captured in a written account of the Apostle Paul's personal experience. In a letter to the Romans, Paul writes the following:

> "We know that the law is spiritual; but I am
> unspiritual, sold as a slave to sin. 15 I do not understand
> what I do. For what I want to do I do not do, but what I
> hate I do. 16 And if I do what I do not want to do, I agree
> that the law is good. 17 As it is, it is no longer I myself who
> do it, but it is sin living in me. 18 For I know that good itself
> does not dwell in me, that is, in my sinful nature. For I
> have the desire to do what is good, but I cannot carry it
> out. 19 For I do not do the good I want to do, but the evil I
> do not want to do—this I keep on doing. 20 Now if I do what
> I do not want to do, it is no longer I who do it, but it is sin
> living in me that does it. 21 So I find this law at
> work: Although I want to do good, evil is right there with
> me. 22 For in my inner being I delight in God's law; 23 but I

> see another law at work in me, waging war against the law of my mind and making me a prisoner of the law of sin at work within me. 24 What a wretched man I am! Who will rescue me from this body that is subject to death? 25 Thanks be to God, who delivers me through Jesus Christ our Lord! So then, I myself in my mind am a slave to God's law, but in my sinful nature a slave to the law of sin". [13]

There is an ongoing battle within the believer between the spirit man and the soul. The things that the soul has been exposed to before they believed for salvation and are awakened from the dead into a newness of life, continue to interfere with the new revelation of Jesus Christ and new life in Him. The mind has been well-taught and formed in its ways and how it responds to life in general. This new way of the Lord remains foreign to the soul or the mind unless there is a continued renewal of the mind for transformation to fully take place. Paul overcame the struggle and he shows us how he did. First, it is in his big thanks to Jesus Christ our Lord.

The victory is in the acknowledgement of the finished work of Christ and in reckoning us as dead to sin according to the Word of the Lord. There is no new sacrifice or offering that will stop the power of sin except that which has been offered once and for all by Christ. The next secret to the victory of Paul is in the Law of the Spirit of life in Christ Jesus. It is a law that is responsible for constant failings, now the victory came by a new law. The first law

13 Romans 7:14, NKJV

is the law of sin and death. This is the law that introduces and causes an awareness of sin without supplying the power to overcome it. All it does is give sin prominence and by it the power of sin increases. This may explain why no human legislation has ever put an end to the increase of crime, but a city-wide revival did.

The law has no power to stop sin, rather it gives sin more power through consciousness. The consciousness of sin is the power of sin. Children are great examples of this. Children get introduced to sin and wrongdoing many times by the warning of what not to touch, and then suddenly their curiosity is awakened and all they want to do is touch what they have been warned not to touch. The instruction has no grace in it, and it does not give the child the power to say no to the urge to do what they ought not to do. There is however a law that works contrary to the law of sin and death; it is the Law of the Spirit of Life in Christ Jesus.

Like the Law of Gravity and the Law of Aerodynamics, it takes one law to defy and to suspend the other. So, when the Law of Aerodynamics is applied and is operation, the aero plane is exempt from the Law of Gravity. It takes a law to be free from the power of other laws. The same is applicable in the human judicial system. It is by a law that a person is condemned to die, and it takes another law also for the same prisoner now to be freed and pardoned by the President of the United States. It is the law to which you submit that you will be governed by. A man does not obey the law he is a slave to, it is because he obeys and responds to that law that he becomes a slave to that law.

Paul, the Apostle puts it this way; "Don't you know that when you offer yourselves to someone as obedient slaves, you are slaves of the one you obey-whether you are slaves to sin, which leads to death, or to righteousness, which leads to righteousness" (**Romans 6:16**). It is your obedience and response to the law that subjects you as slave to it. The word translated "set free" in **Romans 8:2**, is also the word "release from" or "exempted". So, the deliverance from sin does not wipe off the rule of sin and death, but it exempts the subscribers from the rule of sin and death. The law of sin and death still exists but those who believe in Christ must realize that they have been divinely exempted from its rule and control.

In the United States there are laws that apply to Resident Aliens that do not apply to United States citizens and there are other laws that affect non-immigrant visitors that do not affect those who are Legal Permanent Residents and citizens even though they live in the same country. We are in the world, but we are not of the world. We are not under the law to fulfill all it requires, its demands and laws, but we are under grace because Jesus Christ has already fulfilled all the requirements of the Law for us and as us. The redeemed soul has no obligation to respond to life according to how everyone else does. He does not fear what the world fears and how they fear. He is spiritually minded; he views all things from the perspective of the Spirit and does not consider things by their earthly values and situations.

Who Drives Your Emotions?

The life that is governed by the Law of the Spirit of life in Christ Jesus will be spiritually minded, that is, we focus and set our minds on the realities of the finished work of Christ and the ongoing work of the Holy Spirit in us rather than on the things happening all around us. We begin to live by a different rule; we live responding to the dictates of the Spirit and living from the inside out. The one who lives according to the flesh, is subject to the law of sin and death and has allowed themselves to be held bound by the limitations of the flesh. They are enslaved by their innate ungodly desires. Whoever governs the mind, controls the emotions.

Cain's Complex: How it All Begins

The enemy invaded the life of Cain by attacking his emotions first. His face was downcast, and he was angry. So, God spoke, "Then the LORD said to Cain, "Why are you angry? Why is your face downcast? If you do what is right, will you not be accepted? But if you do not do what is right, sin is crouching at your door; it desires to have you, but you must rule over it."

Master It or It Will Own You

Fair warning! God told Cain about sin crouching at his door. The word crouch is used to describe a lion lying in wait to bounce on its prey. He does so quietly in order not to scare its prey away or create any suspicion until the right moment when he can devour and devastate; the opportune moment it has been waiting for.

Sin is as deadly as a crouching lion. There was once a horrific video of a circus owner who used to perform with a lion. The lions were well tamed and were so used to him, but on one unsuspecting day, while on their way to the circus, one of the lions got hold of its owner and pinned him down with his jaws on his arm in the glare of watching assistants and the circus crew.

Unchecked emotions are potential deadly sins; they are like lions being raised in the home for domestication. The lion is a wild animal cut for the wild and not for domestication. There is no way to dress sin into acceptable behavior, it will devour and still cause death nonetheless, it is a matter of time. But before it becomes a devouring lion, it must be checked as a cub of emotions.

God's warning came with clear instructions on what to do

to the brewing emotion. Master it! If he could not master it, God would not have told him to master it. It is because Cain's emotion could be mastered, that was why God instructed him to master the sin that is crouching at this door. The attitude of helplessness to emotions is not totally true. Everyone can tame their emotions and keep them under control.

One of the ministries of the Holy Spirit in the believer's life is to help them to bring their soul under the governance of the Spirit. One vital part of the fruit of the Spirit is self-control or temperance; this is the ability to keep your temper or temperament under the governance and Lordship of the Spirit of Christ. A man without self-control is like a city without wall. One of the scary things about uncontrolled emotions is that they grow to become the master and they hold men in bondage.

There are many people who are locked up in the prison of their own souls because of untamed emotions. The emotional feeling of lust that is not surrendered will destroy its container, their destiny, and the destinies of the people around them. Anger is another example of an emotion that begins innocently and grows into full-blown hatred and hatred grows into murder. The Bible teaches to be angry but not sin and not allow anger to linger till sundown. This means that all negative emotions must be dealt with quickly and decisively. When you are angry, do not let the anger dictate what you will do next. You make it the governor over your own emotions when you do.

Cain had negative emotions and God caught it early and warned him about it, but Cain did not catch it and did not heed the warning. His face fell as he was in a depressive mood. A mood of sadness is another breeding ground for evil. Whatever is after your joy is after your life. Do not let anything or anyone put you into a sad mood. Do everything you can to flee from every appearance of evil. You can know when sin is at your door by the state of your emotions.

Evil has a smell, you cannot but know him when he's around. Every time there is loss of joy, there is the evil one at the door. Stinky trash won't need any special announcement or invitation sent out to flies. The flies are attracted to stinky trash just as evil and a demonic presence is attracted to negative emotions. You can use your emotion to glorify God or you can use them to honor the devil; your response is everything. Everyone will be tempted. Thoughts will fly like birds over a man's head, but they must not be allowed to build a nest on his head.

Things will go wrong around us, but we must never let evil get in our head. You cannot stop the birds from flying over your head, but you can surely stop the birds from building nests on your head. Godly living involves the intentional practice of saying no to the suggestions of the enemy that come to our minds beginning with thoughts. Thoughts develop into desires, and desires into strong emotions, and emotions into will, and will into action. Keep the helmet of salvation on your head and in your mind. This is a constant consciousness of the truth of redemption, crucified with

Christ, dead to sin and the world, alive to God and alive unto righteousness.

All negative emotions announce the likely invasion of the enemy in your life. They will always usher in deadly sins. The feelings of hate, anger, bitter envy, jealousy, anxiety, depression, worry, and fear are a few negative emotions. These will always open a person up to mightier sins than themselves. Some are not sin in themselves, but they are like stench that will attract the deadly flies of sin. The best thing always is to master these emotions as soon as they surface because they can open one up to a lifetime of struggle and frustration.

Dealing with Negative Emotions

God said to Cain, you must master it! This means that every time there is sin at your door, there is one cure that is God-prescribed: Master it! One can practically deal with any negative emotion by following these steps.

I. Set Watch Over Your Gates

The first thing you need to do to master sin is to set a watch over your gates. The two major gates to the heart are our ears and our eyes. Other gates are all of your other senses. I remember many years ago as a teenager who had been following God for about 5 years then, I visited one of our sisters in her parents' house and when we entered, the doors were not usually locked, so anyone could walk in, thanks to the village life. We walked in, and to the left was a room, where our beautiful sister in the Lord was ironing clothes and she was wearing a tank top that left most of her body exposed.

While my flesh would like to feast on this gorgeous body of God's lovely creature, my spirit knew there was something of greater value to my soul than such a feast. I looked straight ahead and went directly to the living room while she tried to cover up. My other brother who had walked into the house with me actually went into the ironing room and I still do not know how he managed, but I do not joke with my eye-gates. No one really falls into sin; most people usually walk into it by not setting guard over their gates.

Proverbs 4:23 says, "Above all else, guard your heart, for everything you do flows from it". The responsibility to guard the heart is a priority and it is of life related importance. Whatever dominates your heart and mind will dominate your life. So, guard your heart and give it all it takes to do it. Watch what you see and what you hear, and you will sift what you permit into your heart that might begin to tickle your soul and excite it with negative emotions.

II. Know Your Priorities

The second thing to do to master your emotions is to understand priorities. Consider the cost of a flared-up emotion and what you stand to gain or lose in the process. Estimate the gains compared to what you stand to lose whenever you choose to express your emotions. Somethings are just not worth the sacrifice. Place high value on relationships with people more than your personal 'good feelings'. Healthy, growing relationships with the people around you are worth a million times more than a moment of ill-feelings caused by a wound.

People have sacrificed their marriages, business partnerships, and ministry impact for a 'good feeling'. Place higher priorities on your relationships with your spouse, your siblings, your parents, your friends, and work or business associates. With the right value placed on relationships, the chances of emotional outbursts reduce because there is an ability to process the emotional expressions according to the value attached to each relationship.

People are not their actions. Actions are events and incidences. Learn to separate what happened from who you are. Most times people dwell too long on a matter of the past that they begin to be united with the circumstances of their lives. They think they are a failure because they failed often in the past. They think they are pain because they have caused much pain and people have called them so.

People identify with their illnesses and diseases, and they become one with the diseases that they are almost beginning to answer to the name of the diseases and become sensitive whenever the sickness is mentioned. They have grown an affinity and affection for what they did not like. They never liked it, yet they have formed an emotional attachment to it.

There are people who grew up with abusive parents and as much as they never liked the way they were treated by their own parents, they end up just like their parents because they have allowed the incidents and the feeling it gave them to become a lingering feeling and they have given it so much thought that they have become what they hated.

III. Set Your Priorities

Thirdly, place higher priority on your goal of righteousness, love, peace, and joy. Directing focus on positive attitudes and characters; positive outcomes and emotions of joy, peace, righteousness, and love become desired outcomes in all decisions. Develop an attitude that loves these feelings and the outcomes they bring to you personally and to the people around you. As this new desire for positive emotions grows, a new sense of value for those positive feelings and outcomes become of greater value and worth.

Therefore, you will not sacrifice your personal righteousness, social peace, and spiritual joy for a moment of emotional outburst. So, when the trigger is pulled, you weigh the value of your outburst against the value of what might be lost in the process, and this estimation happens gradually and consistently until it becomes a new natural response to all emotional triggers.

IV. Heal

Fourth, submit to a healing process. Time doesn't heal, time reveals. Many wounds that seem to be healed with time were usually just in hibernation because with the guns still loaded it will take a trigger to realize that even though much time had passed, the hurt resurfaces when a similar incident looms or happens.

V. Reset Your Mind

Renew your mind by setting it sin renewal mode by the Word of God. Exchange your thoughts for the thoughts of God and deliberately and intentionally shift the focus of your thoughts on God's thought as related to every thought that comes across your mind. This is how to bring every thought captive when the thoughts try to exalt themselves above the knowledge of God in our minds. This means also that the knowledge of God must continue to grow to such heights that cannot be easily surpassed by anything else.

VI. Identify the Triggers

Take time to identify the emotions you need to master and identify the trigger-event or people that excite them. Name the emotion. For Cain, God called it sadness. Then God queried for the trigger when He asked Cain, "Why are you sad?" An honest answer to that is the process of identifying the trigger of the sad emotional Cain was feeling.

VII. Trace the Initial Point of Conditioning

It is helpful to unravel the initial event that caused a repeated pattern of emotional outbursts. This is most important when it has to do with a trauma. The goal is to surrender the memory of that event to the Lordship of Jesus Christ. Let him take that burden off you. Cast all your cares and burdens upon Him for He cares for you. This calls for intentionality.

Identify the specific burden and emotional worries and cares that you need to take off your heart so that the Lordship of Jesus may be permitted over it. Hatred for a person may be initiated by the offense of a person like them. A wife's hatred for the husband may be generated from the trauma they underwent in the hand of an abusive father for example. So, trying to deal with hatred towards their husband without carefully isolating it from the hatred coming from traumatic abuse of the father will not bring lasting healing.

VIII. Tackle Your Desires

Try to understand your desire and dissect it. What do you really want? What do you really need? What do you really expect to satisfy that desire? For example, sexual emotion is not usually a want or an actual need. The real need may be affection or affirmation or a need for acceptance which may appear to be satisfied by sex but in actual reality will not. True satisfaction comes from being loved and feeling needed and valued rather than having sex. Killing Abel did not satisfy the emotional desires of Cain. Killing his brother could never quench the desire to be accepted by God, but he was deceived because he didn't tackle and understand what his real needs were.

IX. Set New Goals

Now that you have learned what your true needs and desires are, and prayerfully those needs and desires are rooted in the word and will of God for your life, you need to set new goals.

Setting new goals will keep you focused and provide you with a detailed plan for goals achievement.

For example, an angry person will ask, what is the goal? Respect. How do you achieve the desired respect? Anger outburst that make you slap or speak rashly to the other people may only worsen the situation and you become even more disrespected than if you had employed a different means of expression, such as dialogue.

X. Use Your Words

Learn to adopt kingdom dialogue. Dialogue is a two-way means of expression of your emotions. You talk and listen to the other person talk. Using your words does not imply that words do not hurt. Words can kill and hurt really badly. This is not what is implied here. Talk with people. Do not just talk to or at them.

Express your thoughts in words more than in feelings and in Christ-thought-processed actions. Use your words to achieve your set goals and desired outcomes. Use your words in ways that get you the respect you want to fight for, not in ways that make you lose more respect than ever.

XI. Develop Kingdom Thoughts

We do not just have the Spirit of God and of Christ indwelling us as believers, we also have the mind of Christ. So, we must permit this mind to be in us as it was in Christ Jesus. We must be in touch with the indwelling Christ in us. You are driving and you have a passenger in the back seat. You can talk to them without having to look at them. Although you do not see them, they are there. This is how Christ indwells us. He resides in us in a way we may not see him, yet we have a consciousness and total awareness of His indwelling presence within us. We talk to him because we know He is there and take our thoughts to Christ in us and let Him think through our mind.

The right thoughts develop in concert with His nature while the wrong thoughts are burned up and destroyed in the holiness of His thoughts. This is how to practice the mind of Christ. Engage the Spirit of God in your thought process.

Stubborn Emotions Require Drastic Measures

One would wonder why a man can hear clear warnings even from God and the next step they take is to go in the exact direction that they were warned against? Cain went ahead and yielded to the dark emotion of hatred and murdered his own brother. This shows that the control of man is not outside him, but it is in him. God cannot help a man who is not willing to receive help. This is why the Bible says, "...as many as received him and believed in his name, to them He gave the power to become children of God," **(John 1:12)**. Just like the remote-control only works when the device itself is powered up; God does not force his will on man because of the freewill, which he gave man so that man may freely yield his will to God in all he chooses.

Master It by the Word of God

We must be in sync with God infusing ourselves with his words. Jesus said, 'If ye **abide** in me, and my words **abide** in you, ask whatsoever ye will, and it shall be done unto you' **(John15:7)**. The word outside us has no power over us like the word inside us. Read the word, speak the word, meditate on the word, believe the word, confess the word, obey the word, and do the word. Let the word of Christ dwell in you richly in all wisdom until the word of God begins to shape your world.

Master It by Knowledge of Your Resources

Man is a more powerful entity than we realize. So, God

turns the lives of men from the inside out. You will always gravitate toward your most dominant thoughts and desires. Discover that God has given you great and mighty resources all around you to help in times of need. His divine power has given us all things that we may ever need for life and godliness. Seek help, find someone to talk to and relate with.

Quickly forgive those who hurt you. Do not intentionally estrange yourself from people. Keep them close before you will need them, so they are easy to approach when the need resources. Explore the resources of the Word, and prayer, and of the fellowship with other believers.

Be Your Brother's Keeper

No matter how far man is from God, it is the pleasure of God to keep Himself in man's consciousness always. God created man to be able to master every other created thing including man's emotions. Emotions are created so that man may use them to honor and glorify God on the earth. Beware of anger and other negative emotions, they open a door to greater sins and evil. Do not give room for negative emotions to linger, they are not worth losing the presence of God for. You can only conquer your emotions by the word of God dwelling in you, not the word around you. The emotion you do not conquer will not only impact you, but it will also impact the people around you.

Where Is Your Brother?

God places people in our lives for a purpose; our lives are inter-connected. God makes men responsible for one another (**Ezekiel 33:1-6**).

How Am I Responsible for Another Man's Life?

- **Interconnectedness**. we are connected one to another. What happens to one affects the other. There are people whose destiny are attached to the fulfilment of your destiny. This means that if you do not get yourself together, you will not be able to impact these people's destinies and impact them towards God. What you do or refuse to do determines the destiny of others.
- **Presence**. The invisible God is present in the visible man; we are God's representative. From Adam to the last Adam, Jesus Christ, we are created and redeemed to represent God in bodily form. There are things men would never know of God unless they see Him in and through us as we live our lives to reveal Him in love, faith, compassion, and power.
- **Ownership + stewardship in relationship.** There is a false idea about relationship where people assume ownership over other people's lives. Parents do not own their children; husbands do not own their spouse. God is the owner of all men and all lives. No one, therefore, has a right to hurt another or to take the life of another. A pregnant woman does not own the life that is growing inside her to the point that she can terminate that life in claim of ownership. All that we are and will ever be, are stewards. God commits people's lives to us, as parents, children, spouses, and

friends. We must be responsible to take care of everyone God has placed in our lives.

God is the ultimate keeper of life, but he has committed so much power to man to take care of the earth and for Him and for one another. God gives man leadership and stewardship not ownership. You are responsible for your relationships. We cannot be unconcerned for the plight of the people in our life.

The ignorance of your position in people's lives is not an excuse to not keep them. Understand your place in peoples' lives. Understand the impact and implication of your action or inaction in people's lives. You are not God, but you may represent God in many people's lives.

What Have You Done?

Responsibility means doing something for the life of others. You cannot be responsible and do nothing. What you do goes a long way to preserve destiny or to pervert it. You are either killing them or keeping them from being killed. Hatred and anger, as well as other negative emotions kill and destroy people's lives and do not build. Every hater is a potential murderer. The good Samaritan teaches us a great lesson on who a neighbor is (**Luke 10:29-37**).

There are people you meet in the journey of life that even though you may have met by chance, there is a divine purpose for you to fulfill in their life and you cannot allow your emotions to get in the way of you fulfilling that divine purpose. There is a neighbor in whose life you must play the role of a keeper for God. There are people that God will rightly require at your hand.

There are people whose salvation and rescue from the power of darkness and evil you should be committed to. As God asked Cain a question and he lied, he said, "I do not know, am I my brother's keeper?" There would be no need to cover up when you are committed to the assignment you have been given to keep. Your emotions affect everyone around you in very major ways; your emotions may be killing when it yields action or inaction, or it may help you keep someone safe.

10

Kingdom Thought Process.

All emotions are originated or fueled in the thought-realm. When there is a loss of life of a close associate or family member, the grief gets deeper as thoughts begins to get deeper. The thoughts of how the loss could have been avoided; thoughts of shared memorable moments that are gone forever; the tragic loss and how the mind replays the scenes of what happened and so on. This is a thought-fueled emotion. The grief occurred because of a loss, and the emotion continues to run and run deeper as the thought gets deeper.

The same goes for worries. The thoughts continue to brood on possibilities and run in circles about what could be and what may never be. The enemy attacks the emotions by gaining access to the thought realm. The devil has access to the soul realms of man including believers to suggest thoughts and plants seeds of images in the imagination. Paul describes the thought realm as the stronghold that must be pulled down and dismantled. "The weapons of our warfare are not carnal, but they are mighty through God to the pulling down of strongholds, casting down imagination and every high that exalts itself against the knowledge of God, and bringing into captivity every thought to the obedience of Christ" (**2 Corinthians 10:4-5**).

The strongholds Paul wrote about are not some shrine of witches and wizards set up by some idol worshippers. Rather, Paul wrote about the thoughts, knowledge, concepts, and belief systems, imaginations and thoughts or thinking patterns that permit the enemy to interrupt the flow of God's grace, power, and love in and through us as we live to give God's glory full expression in the earth. A stronghold is a place that has been fortified so as to protect it against attack. It is a place where a particular cause or belief is strongly defended or upheld. The best picture of a stronghold is a defensive structure usually set up by an army in times of war where they secure all their ammunition and their base for retreats and reloading.

Once the enemy can figure out where the stronghold of their opposition army is, once a stronghold is captured, the war is over and won. The army whose stronghold is pulled down only fights their last because they have no way to reload or retreat. This is what the enemy does in his attack against every single person on the earth. He builds strongholds in the mind and loads them with thoughts ahead of the real battle, so he is not only fighting from outside, he is fighting from within also because he has built a stronghold in the mind in form of thoughts, imaginations, ideas, and beliefs.

The nature of the thoughts that the enemy depends upon in building his strongholds are thoughts, imaginations, traditions, and beliefs that exalt themselves or are set against the knowledge of God. Thoughts that are contrary to the thoughts of God, and traditions that are opposed to the ways of God. The Holy Spirit aligns our thoughts with his thoughts and our ways with His ways. This is the process of pulling down strongholds and casting down imaginations. We exchange our thoughts for His thoughts, so whenever a thought comes in the head region, we bring that thought down in obedience to the obedience of Christ, and we force it into alignment. This is what I call, kingdom thought process.

There are two possible thought processes, the head thought process and the heart thought process. The regenerated heart has an advantage of downloading the thoughts into a region of a regenerated heart. This is the place where God processes His thoughts in us. God has thoughts that he thinks towards us, we need to know that thought and bridge the gap between His thoughts and our thoughts. When we think in the head region, the thoughts generate more emotional anxieties, worries and fears. The goal is to give every thought to Christ within us. We think with the mind of Christ and this is how we put the Satanic and worldly thought flow out.

We have the mind of Christ, and thoughts of evil cannot survive the mind of Christ. The reason we read, study, and meditate on the word of God is because the word of God are His thoughts. We think every thought with the mind of Christ and with the Spirit of Christ within us. Every thought goes through this sifting process where we force them to obey Christ's principles and not permit any thought to be exalted above the knowledge of God.

Paul writes, "Finally Brethren, whatsoever things are true, whatsoever things are honest, whatsoever things are just, whatsoever things are pure, whatsoever things are lovely, whatsoever things are of good report; if there be any virtue, and if there be any praise, think on these things," **(Philippians 4:8)**. This is the kingdom thought process.

Be selective of what you think. Never permit any thought to linger in the heart and mind when they do not fit in. Paul's recommended character of the thoughts to think about. Select the thoughts with the consciousness of the presence of the Holy Spirit in your heart and the sweet voice of the Spirit of Christ.

Negative thoughts will fuel negative emotions; kingdom thoughts will breed kingdom emotions of peace and joy in the Holy Ghost (**Romans 14:17**). We subject and subdue thoughts as they come to the obedience of Christ. Thought flows are practically alterable by speaking out loud and this helps to take charge of thought flow by altering it with confession of the Word of God each time. We bring panicky thoughts into the realm of peaceful thoughts; we bring painful thoughts into the realm of comforting thoughts.

Take No Thought

The Kingdom thought process also involves taking no thoughts at all. Many times, emotions run wild because we take too much thought of everything than we ought to. So, Jesus recommended that we may take no thought at all for tomorrow, what we will eat, what we will wear, what will happen, and will not happen.

Taking no thoughts at all is an extraordinarily strong place of peace to be. It is a place of total surrender and total relaxation; no fretting, no trying, just trusting and relaxing. It is a place of total flow in the river of God's peace and joy.

11

Afterword: The Motive of Love.

I am going to talk to you now, about three types of generations: The Cain Generation, the Abel Generation and the Love Generation.

The Cain Generation

There's a Cain generation and spirit still at work in men today. Anger, envy, jealousy, hatred, shame, regrets, doubts, fear, murder and murderous intentions are still emotions that the enemy is ravishing the lives of men with today perpetuating Cain against Abel. This spirit of Cain must be expelled from the church and not permitted to thrive anymore.

The Abel Generation

The Abel generation is the faith generation, the righteous generation. His blood cried when he was murdered from under the earth. The voice of Abel could not be silent even in death. Those who think that death is the end are grossly mistaken. There are people who cannot die; you may kill them, but their voice will yet speak.

Abel was a voice man, and everyone who is a voice that is heaven sent is always open to the attack of the spirit of Cain. You are a voice that cannot afford to be silenced before its time. Love is everything that overcomes the Spirit of Cain. Cain could have been rescued from the eternal punishment he received if he had conquered hate by love. Love is what placed the voice of Abel in the position of power over the murderous spirit of Cain.

The Love Revolution

The reason we care is love. Love only and love always will be the right motive for which to be mindful of other people's emotions and how your emotion may impact and affect your life and their lives. We may undo the spirit of Cain with the Spirit of love. The spirit of Cain reveals an unacceptable character; he had a habitual lifestyle that made him a person who was not acceptable to God.

The spirit of Cain is also revealed in its concerns; the emotions are symptoms of bigger issues; they are the signs that the devil is around the corner. The spirit of Cain is careless about the feelings and destinies of others. The care for self only and not for others is a dangerous attitude for anyone. We are called to care for the total wellbeing of one another.

The Spirit of Cain comes with serious consequences. The consequences can be too hard for anyone to bear. Cain was banished from the favor and the presence of God, and he was banished from rest and peace of mind and became a prey waiting to be destroyed. John warns in **1 John 3:12** "Do **not be like Cain**, who belonged to the evil one and murdered his brother. And why did he murder him? Because his own actions were evil and his brothers were righteous.

John alerts us that there is a potential repetition of the experience of Cain in the church today. Emotions that are untamed that cause death because of jealousy, envy and strife; the feeling of hate of one brother and sister to another; the jealousy of the elder sons in the Father's house of the returning prodigals who were lost and dead but now are found, and alive, and celebrated by the Father with lavished grace. Love must remain our motive. Hate leads to murder, and murder will cause those who were born as God's gift to mankind to become the devil's own, because they failed to subdue the emotions and the yearnings of their flesh to the light of God and of His love.

I never liked vampire movies, but I have watched a couple of them in my teenage years. One of the vampire movies I watched showed the vampires active in the cover of darkness and they are destroyed when exposed to rays of light. In the same way, negative emotions, like vampires must be exposed to light, the light of Christ's principles and of Christ's presence will destroy the growing desires and emotions of hate, fear, and doubts.

Those who are suffering from more chronic emotions of depression and anger will find liberty when those who are around them love on them and not judge them too harshly. It is the spirit of Cain that makes us view those who are not as strong in faith as we are or as consistent in their walk as we are to be enemies. The spirit of Cain converts friends and brothers into enemies, but the Spirit of Love converts even enemies into brothers and friends in the kingdom.

Believers love and do not kill the one that has been gravely wounded by the enemy in their battle of life. We support and become our brother's keepers. We lift those who fall and allow them to climb on our back into greater heights to the glory of our Father. Even Cain still found mercy in the eternal love of God, a mark was placed upon him so that he would not die or be hurt by any man who found him. It is because he was already a wounded man.

Cain's Punishment and Pardon

Cain lamented that the punishment for his sin was too great to bear. One would think Cain was a hardened criminal who will never break, but no, not under the weight of God's judgment. He was a tiller of the ground, but the ground he lives to till will no longer yield its strength to him. The cursed ground still yielded to Cain despite the Adam curse in the fall, but now it will no longer because it received the blood of his brother and it was Cain's fault. Even the ground is sane enough to understand justice. Do not think that the elements of the earth don't listen and watch as witnesses against men who perpetuate evil in the glare of these invisible witnesses. Life in its entirety is spiritual. Be careful what you do in the watch of the sun or the moon or the earth. Be careful what you give them, they have ability to respond accordingly.

Jesus spoke about the dust of the feet of his disciples as a witness against those who refuse to accept the message of peace and eternal salvation they bring.

Made in the USA
Las Vegas, NV
29 December 2024

15579152R00056